Divide and Conquer Algorithms for Multi-dimensional Problems

Aditya Chatterjee

K. Sai Drishya

Benjamin QoChuk

This book not only present algorithms and analysis of advanced real-life problems but also prepares you to have a deep understanding of how these algorithms were originally designed and an ability to solve some of the most insightful algorithmic problems.

Table of Contents

All problem consists of 1-dimension problem, 2-dimension problem, 3-dimension problem, k-dimension problem (all with time complexity analysis) and real-life applications.

Introduction

Multidimensional divide and conquer is an algorithmic technique that can be used to develop several algorithms and data structures for multi-dimensional problems. It is an extension of Divide and Conquer algorithms which is usually applied for 1 dimensional data.

The basic idea of Divide and Conquer is to divide the problem into smaller problems, solve the smaller problems and use the answers from the smaller problems to get the answer to the larger problem.

Merge Sort is a popular algorithm that applies **Divide and Conquer to sort 1-dimensional data**.

Extending such algorithms for Multi-dimensional data is not simple but it is an interesting approach that which nurture your thinking process.

This is important as most real-life problems are multi-dimensional like:

- A map of Earth is a 2-dimensional data
- Text is a multi-dimensional data for Clustering problems
- Augmented reality is usually 3-dimensional data
- Game graphics are at-least 3-dimensional data

- Physics consider our **Universe to be 11-dimensional data**

We use this paradigm to give best-known solutions to problems such as:

- ECDF
- Maxima
- Range searching
- Closest pair
- All nearest neighbor problems.

Introduction to Divide and Conquer

Divide and Conquer is an algorithmic technique based on recursively dividing a sub problem and using the solutions of those to solve the original one. Examples include many algorithms such as Binary Search, Merge Sort and Quick Sort.

It is a known fact that algorithm design and analysis has made many contributions to the field of computer science of both theoretical and practical significance. A research has begun laying the **groundwork for a theory of algorithm design** by identifying certain algorithmic methods that are used in the solution of a wide variety of problems.

Almost all of the algorithmic paradigms that had been discussed to date are at one of two extremes:

- they are so general that they cannot be discussed precisely
- they are so specific that they are useful in solving only one or two problems.

A more "**middle of the road**" paradigm that can be precisely specified and yet can also be used to solve many problems in its domain of applicability is called multidimensional divide-and-conquer.

Definition

To solve a problem of N points in k-space (k dimensional space), first **recursively solve two problems each of N/2 points in k-space**, and then **recursively solve one problem of N points in (k-1)-dimensional space**.

In this article we are going to look at various algorithms such as ECDF, maxima, range searching, closest pair and all nearest neighbor problems and see how each one can be viewed as an instance of **multidimensional divide and conquer**.

There are three distinct benefits from such a study:

1. A coherent presentation as such makes the **description of the algorithm to be communicated more easily.**

2. When we study algorithms in a group, **advances made on one can be transferred to another problem**.

3. If clearly understood, the paradigm can **help us solve unsolved research problems**.

1. Domination Problems

A **point domination** can be defined as the point A dominates a point B when A_i the ith coordinate of point A dominates point B if and only if $A_i > B_i$ for all i, $l <= i <= k$.

If two points, let us say A and B, do not dominate each other, then we can that they are **incomparable**. It is clear from these definitions that the dominance relation defines a partial ordering (consider this as sorting) on any k-dimensional point set.

These concepts are illustrated for the case k = 2 in below figure. The point A dominates the point B, and both pairs A, C and B, C are incomparable.

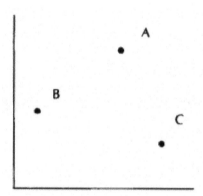

1.1 Empirical Cumulative Distribution Functions (ECDF)

In statistics the empirical cumulative distribution function (ECDF) for a sample set S of N elements, evaluated at point x, is just **rank(x)/N**. Given a set S of N points we define the **rank of point x to be the number of points in S dominated by x**.

Since ECDF is related to rank, we often write **ECDF for rank**. With this notation we can state **two important computational problems**.

1. **All-Points ECDF**: Given a set S of N points in k-space, compute the rank of each point in the set.

2. **ECDF Searching**: Given a set S, organize it into a data structure such that queries of the form "what is the rank of point x" can be answered quickly (where x is not necessarily an element of S).

1.1.1 All-Points ECDF problem

As mentioned above the problem requires the rank of each point in a set S of N points in k-space. We will start with the one dimensional problem and then gradually, increase the dimensions.

One-dimensional all-points ECDF

If k=1, this would be a simple list and to find rank of any number, we would have sorted the list and the index of the element is the rank (0 based indexing). Hence, a sorting algorithm would be optimal for one-dimensional with **running time of O(N logN)**.

Consider this list **[2, 5, 0, 9, 4]**

If we sort the list, we get [0, 2, 4, 5, 9]

The rank of an element is the index of that element in the sorted list. For example, rank of 4 is 2.

Hence, ECDF of element 4 is 2/5 (as there are 5 elements) = 0.4

Similarly, ECDF of each element can be calculated in constant time.

Hence, the main operation of one dimensional ECDF is sorting which is a well-studied domain and can be solved in **O(N log N) time**.

Two-dimensional all-points ECDF

Now the same problem in two-dimensional can get a little trickier. Hence, we use multi-dimensional divide and conquer for it. Recalling the definition that says to solve a problem of N points in k-space, first recursively solve two problems each of N/2 points in k-space, and then recursively solve one problem of N points in (k-1)-dimensional space.

Our planar ECDF algorithm operates as follows.

1) The **first step is to choose some vertical line L dividing the point set S into two subsets A and B**, each containing N/2 points, illustrated in the figure below.

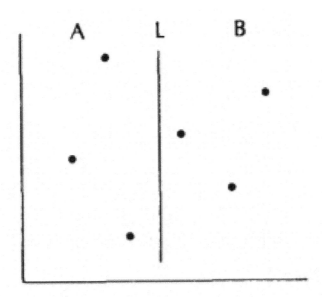

2) The **second step of our algorithm calculates for each point in A its rank among the points in A**, and likewise the rank of each point in B among the points of B, illustrated in the figure below.

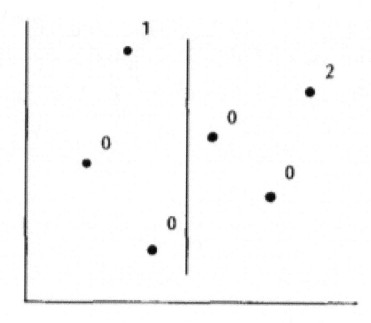

An important observation can be made here which allows us to combine these sub-solutions efficiently to form a solution to the original problem. Since every point in A has an x-value less than every point in B, two facts hold:

1. No point in A dominates any point in B

2. A point b in B dominates point a in A if and only if the **y-value of b is greater than the y-value of a**.

By the first fact, we know that the ranks we computed for A are the correct final ranks. We still need to calculate for every point in B the number of points it dominates in A which we add to the number of B's it dominates to get the final answer.

To solve this reduced problem, we use the second fact. If we project all the points in S onto the line L (below figure) then can solve the

---

reduced problem by scanning up the line L, keeping track of how many As we have seen, and add that number to the partial rank of each point in B as we pass that point. This counts the number of points in A with smaller y-values, which are exactly the points it dominates. We implement this solution algorithmically by sorting the As and Bs together and then scanning the sorted list.

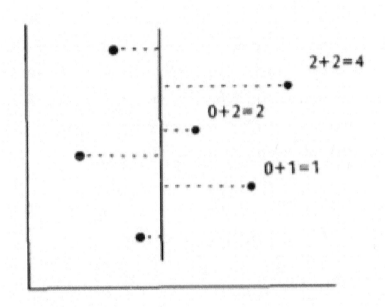

Let us look at formal algorithm that fits the above description. We call it **ECDF2** which is a recursive algorithm that takes set S of N points in the plane and returns the rank of each point as the output

Algorithm ECDF2

1. **Division Step**: If S contains only one element return rank as 0, otherwise proceed by choosing a cut line L perpendicular to the x-axis such that N/2 points of S have x-values less than L's and the remainder have greater values. Note: L is the median x-value of the set.

2. **Recursive Step**: Recursively call ECDF(A), ECDF(B). After this step we know the true ECDF of all points in A.

3. **Marriage Step**: We must now find for each point in B the number of points in A it dominates (i.e., that have lesser y-value) and add this number to its partial ECDF. To do this, pool the points of A and B (remembering their type) and sort them by y-value. Scan through this sorted list in increasing y-value, keeping track in ACOUNT of the number of As so far observed. Each time a B is observed, add the current value of ACOUNT to its partial ECDF.

Time Complexity of 2-dimensional ECDF

Since the algorithm computes rank by induction using the two facts mentioned above, we can also use induction to analyze its running time on a random access computer by forming a recurrence relation describing the running time on N points T(N). To get this, let us consider the number of operations each step of the algorithm requires.

1) **Division step**: This can be solved by fast median algorithm (that sorts the list and picks a median by index); we can use the **algorithm of Blum, called PICK** that finds the ith largest element in a given list in **O(N)** time.

2) Recursion step: Because step 2 solves two problems of size N/2, its cost will be **2 x T(N/2)** by induction.

3) Marriage step: The sort requires O(N log N) time, and the scan requires linear time, so total cost is **O(N log N)**

Now the combined cost is

```
T(N) = O(N) + 2 * T(N/2) + O(N log N)

T(N) = 2 * T(N/2) + O(N log N)

T(N) = O(N * logN * logN)
```

We can make an observation that will allow us to speed up many multi-dimensional divide-and-conquer algorithms. An important thing to notice here is that the running time is dominated by the sort of step 3.

To remove this cost we can sort the N points of S once by-coordinate before any invocation of ECDF2, at a once-for-all cost of O(N lg N). After this we can achieve the effect of sorting (without the cost) by being very careful to maintain "sortedness-by-y" when dividing into sets A and B during step 1.

After this modification, the recurrence describing the modified algorithm becomes:

```
T(N) = 2T(N/2) + O(N)

T(N) = O(N log N)
```

This technique is known as **presorting** and has a very wide range of applicability. Now that we have our algorithm set for N point in two-dimensional, let us see for three-dimensional.

Three-dimensional all-points ECDF

The multi-dimensional divide and conquer that we will apply here is quite like the previous one. The steps of the algorithm are:

1) To solve a problem of N points in 3-space we solve two problems of N/2 points in 3-space and then one problem of N points in 2-space. This step choses a cut plane P perpendicular to the x-axis dividing it into sets A and B of N/2 points each. This is illustrated in the figure below:

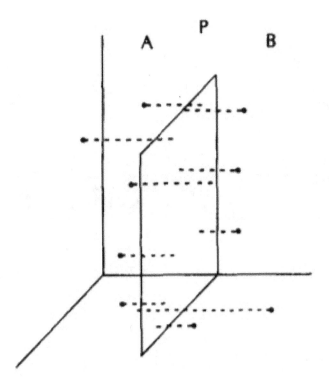

2) Now the algorithm recursively counts for each point in A the number of points in A it dominates, and likewise for B. By the two facts stated above we know that no point in A dominates any point in B, hence the final ranks of A remains same. Ans we know that a point b in B dominates point a in A if and only if b dominates a in their projection on P, the (y, z) plane.

3) The third step projects all points onto plane P and then counts for each B-point the number of A-points it dominates.

Time Complexity of 3-dimensional ECDF

This reduced problem, however, is just a slightly modified version of planar ECDF problem, which can be solved in O(N log N) time. The recurrence describing our three-dimensional algorithm is then

$$T(N) = 2\ T(N/2) + O(N\ \lg N)$$

which, as we saw previously, has solution **T(N) = O(N log^2 N)**.

k-dimensional all-points ECDF

The technique that we just used to solve the two-dimensional and three-dimensional can be extended to solve for k spaces. What we do is, divide into A and B, solve the subproblems recursively, and then patch up the partial answers in B by counting for each point in B the number of As. The (k-1)-dimensional subproblem can be solved by a "bookkeeping" modification to the (k-1)-dimensional ECDF algorithm.

The algorithm can be formally described as:

ECDFk

1. Choose a (k- l)-dimensional cut plane P dividing S into two subsets A and B, each of N/2 points.

2. Recursively call ECDFk(A) and ECDFk(B). After this we know the

---

true ECDF of all points in A.

3. For each B find the number of As it dominates.Project the points of S onto P, noting for each whether it was an A or a B. Now solve the reduced problem using a modified ECDF(k-l) algorithm and add the calculated values to the partial ranks of B.

Time Complexity of k-dimensional ECDF

Let T(N,k) denote the time complexity, Step 1, for any k>2 requires O(N) time, Step 2 takes 2*T(N/2,k) and Step 3 takes T(N,k-1).

```
T(N, k) = O(N) + 2T(N/2, k) + T(N, k-1)

We can use as a basis for induction on k the fact
that

T(N, 2) = O(N log N)

as shown previously, and this establishes that

T(N, k) = O(N log^(k-1) N).
```

Therefore we can conclude that the time taken for an ECDF algorithm for k>1 is **O(N log$^{(k-1)}$N)**.

1.1.2 The ECDF searching problem

In the previous section, we have seen how to find the number of points a given point dominates, in this section we study a related question of whether a given point is dominated. Just like the previous section, we start off with a single dimensional and successively examine higher dimensions.

There are three costs associated with a search structure:

1. **Preprocessing time (P(N))** required to build the structure

2. **Query time (Q(N))** required to search a structure

3. **Storage (S(N))** required to represent the structure in memory.

One-dimensional searching ECDF

The one-dimensional ECDF searching problem asks us to **organize N points (real numbers) such that when given a new point x (not necessarily in the set), we can quickly determine how many points x dominates**.

An obvious solution would involve sorting the points and performing binary search to determine whether x is present, if so, we can simply return its index as it would denote the number of points x dominates.

Time Complexity of 1-dimension searching ECDF

```
P(N) = O(N log N) for sorting

Q(N) = O(log N) for binary search

S(N) = O(N) space complexity for storing the N points
```

Two-dimensional searching ECDF

This involves three steps, thus three costs in total.

Preprocessing Step

In the two-dimensional ECDF searching problem we need to preprocess N points in the plane such that the queries asking the rank of a new point can be answered quickly. There are many data structures that can be handy here, but we focus on ECDF tree which follows the multidimensional divide and conquer paradigm.

The method is similar to the previous section. We divide the N points in 2-dimensional into two subproblems A and B, and one substructure of N points in 1-dimensional. We now describe the top level of an ECDF tree storing the point set S. By analogy to the all-points algorithm, we choose a line L dividing S into equal sized sets A and B.

Instead of solving subproblems A and B, however, we now recursively process them into ECDF trees representing their respective subsets. Now that these subsets are built, we are (almost) prepared to answer ECDF queries in set S.

Query Step

The algorithm starts by comparing the x value of the query point with the line L, there can be two possibilities here, either the point is lesser than L, in this case u , it's rank is calculated by recursively searching the substructure representing A, for obvious reasons we don't consider B. In the other case, that is v, not only do we need the number of points that are being dominated by v, also the points in A that are being dominated by v. The below figure illustrates the above points.

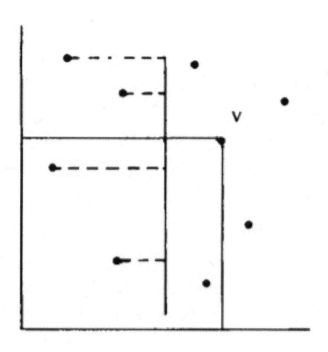

Storage Step

The ECDF tree has internal node representing a set of N points which will contain:

1. x-value (representing the line L)

2. a pointer to a left child (representing A, the N/2 points with

lesser x-values)

3. a right child representing B

4. an array of the N/2 points of A sorted by y-value.

To build the tree, the algorithm recursively divides the set into A and B, builds the subtrees representing each, and then sorts the elements of A by y-value (by presorting). This tree somewhat represents a Binary Search Tree (BST). To search the tree recursively one first compares the x-value of the node with the x-value of the query point. If the query point is less, then only the left child is searched recursively, else the right child. A binary search is done in the sorted y-sequence representing A to find the query point's y rank in A, and the two ranks are added together and returned as the result.

Time Complexity of 2-dimensional searching ECDF

To get a better idea about the search structure, we again use recurrences. We can describe the recurrence relation for the algorithm that performs the preprocessing as

```
Preprocessing step

P(N) = 2P(N/2) + O(N)

We can solve this and get

P(N) = O( N log N)
```

To store an N element set we must store two N/2 element sets plus one sorted list of N/2 elements, so the recurrence is:

```
Storage step

S(N) = 2S(N/2) + N/2

which gives

S(N) = O(N log N)
```

For the search time, our recurrence will depend on whether the point in A or B, and analyze the worst case in which ever set it lies in. Also we must make one comparison, perform a binary search in a structure of size N/2, and then recursively search a structure of size N/2. The cost of this will be

```
Query Step

Q(N) = Q(N/2) + O(log N)

So we know that the worst-case cost of searching is

Q(N) = O(log² N).
```

Now that the planar ECDF tree is done, we can move to higher dimensions.

Three-dimensional searching ECDF

A node representing an N-element ECDF tree in 3- space contains two subtrees (each representing N/2 points in 3-space) and a two-dimensional ECDF tree (representing the projection of the points in A onto the cut plane P) which is built recursively.

The searching algorithm compares the query point's x value to the value defining the cut plane, and if less, searches only the left substructure.

If the query point lies in B, then the right substructure is searched, and a search is done in the two-dimensional ECDF tree.

---

k-dimensional searching ECDF

The full k-dimensional structure is analogous: A node in this structure contains two substructures of N/2 points in k-space, and one substructure of N/2 points in k-1-space.

The recurrences describing the structure containing N points in k-space are

$$P(N, k) = 2P(N/2, k) + P(N/2, k-1) + O(N)$$

$$S(N, k) = 2S(N/2, k) + S(N/2, k-1) + O(1)$$

$$Q(N, k) = Q(N/2, k) + Q(N/2, k-1) + O(1)$$

We can use our previous observations on two-dimensional space as the basis for induction on k. Conclusively we get

$$P(N, k) = O(N \log^{(k-1)} N)$$

$$S(N, k) = O(N \log^{(k-1)} N)$$

$$Q(N, k) = O(\log^k N)$$

Applications of ECDF problem

1. It is often required in statistical applications because it provides a **good estimate of an underlying distribution**, given only a set of points chosen randomly from that distribution.

A common problem include a hypothesis testing of the following form:

Given two point sets, were they drawn from the same underlying distribution?

2. Many important multivariate tests require computing the all-points ECDF problem to answer this question.

3. The solution to the ECDF searching problem is required for certain approaches to **density estimation**, which asks for an estimate of the underlying probability density function given a sample.

Differences between all-points ECDF and searching problem

Both the problems are related although distinct.

In the all-points are required to calculate something about every point in set (Is it dominated? How many points does this dominate?). On the other hand, in searching problem we must organize the data into some

---

structure such that future queries (How many points does this point dominate? Is this point dominated?) may be answered quickly.

Having made these general observations about our primary algorithm design tool, we are ready to apply it to the solution of other problems.

1.2) Maxima

A point is said to be **maxima** if there exists no other point that dominates it. See the below figure of a two-dimensional space representing a set where the maxima have been circled.

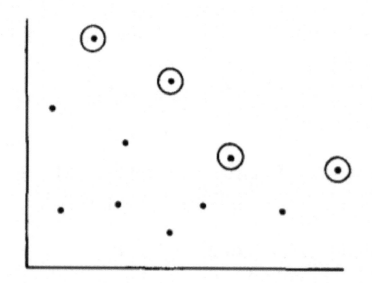

In this section we will be looking into two types of maxima problems

1. **All-points Maxima problem** (given a set, find all maxima).

2. **Searching Maxima problem** (preprocess a set to answer queries asking if a

new point is a maximum of the set).

1.2.1) All-points Maxima problem

Given a set of N points we are required to find all maxima.

One-dimensional all-points maxima

The maxima for a one-dimensional is basically the maximum element in the given set, which can be obtained by exactly comparisons. Computing the maxima of N points in the plane involves the following steps

1. Sort the points into increasing x-order.

2. Scan that sorted list right to left, observing successive "highest y-values so far observed" and marking those as maxima.

The Time Complexity would be **O(N) for the scan** and **O(N log N) for the sort**. We could also develop a multi-dimensional divide and conquer algorithm.

Two-dimensional all-points maxima

Just like before, we divide by L into A and B and solve those subproblems recursively (finding the maxima of each set). This can be seen in the below figure, where the maxima of A have been circled and those of B are in boxes.

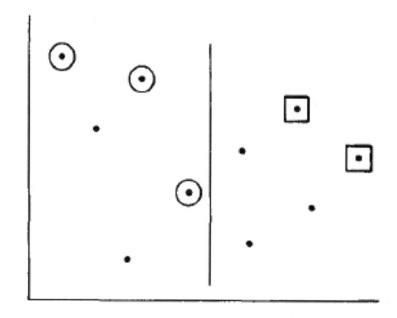

Since no point of B is dominated by any point of A, the maxima of B is the same for the entire set.

The third step ("marriage step") is to discard points of A but not of the whole set. Since all points of B x dominate all the points in A, we need to check for y domination. We therefore project the maxima of A and B onto L, then discard A-points dominated by B-points on the line.

This third step can be easily implemented by just comparing the y-value of all A-maxima with the maximum y-value of the B-maxima and discarding all A's with lesser y-value.

Time Complexity of 2-dimensional all points Maxima

This can be described by the recurrence relation:

$$T(N) = 2T(N/2) + O(N)$$

which has solution **O(N log N)**.

Three-dimensional all-points maxima

We can generalize the previous algorithm to yield results for higher dimensions. The steps include:

1. divide set into A and B,

2. recursively find the maxima of each of those sets

3. discard every maxima of A which is dominated by a maxima of B (since every maxima of B is a maxima of the whole set).

The third step is accomplished by projecting the respective maxima sets onto the plane and then solving the planar problem. We could modify the two-dimensional algorithm to solve this task, but it will be slightly more efficient to use the scanning algorithm.

Suppose we cut into A and B by the z-coordinate; we must discard all As dominated by any Bs in the x-y plane. If we have presorted by x, then we just scan right to left down the sorted list, discarding As with y-values less than the maximum B y-value observed to date.

Time Complexity of 3-dimensional all points Maxima

The running time for marriage step is linear O(N) which includes presorting. Therefore the running time for three-dimensional is same as two-dimensional which is **O(N log N)**.

k-dimensional all-points maxima

For k-space, we do this by solving two problems of N/2 points in k-space and then solving one problem of (up to) N points in (k-1)-space. This reduced problem calls for finding all As in the space dominated by any Bs, and we can solve this by modifying the maxima algorithm (similar to our modifications of the ECDF algorithm).

Time Complexity of K-dimensional all points Maxima

The resulting algorithm has a recurrence:

```
T(N, k) = 2T(N/2, k) + T(N, k-1) + O(N)

We know that T(N, 3) = O(N lg N).
Applying that in the above recurrence, we get

T(N, k) = O(N log^(k-2) N) for k>=3
```

The worst case assumes that all N points of the original set will be the maxima of their subsets, but that is not the case as for many sets, the maxima of A and B will be relatively fewer.

The results from "**On the average number of maxima in a set of vectors and applications**" by J. L. Bentley and H. T. Kung, it was shown that only a very small number of points usually remain maxima for many probability distributions. If only "a very small number of points remain", let us call that number 'm', then

```
T(N, k-1) -> T(m, k-1)
```

For a small enough m (i.e $m = O(N^p)$ for some p<1) has running time O(N). If this is true, then the recurrence relation for the maxima algorithm is:

```
T(N, k) = 2T(N/2, k) + O(N)

T(N) = O(N log N)
```

This running time is the average time for a wide class of distributions.

1.2.2) Maxima Searching

We will start with the 2-dimensional problem as you should have a good idea of solving the 1-dimensional problems based on our previous problems.

Two-dimensional all-points maxima searching

We must process N points in the plane into a data structure so we can quickly determine if a point is maxima. The structure we will use is a binary tree in which the left child of a given node represents all points with lesser x-values (A), the right child represents B, and an x-value represents the line L.

To answer a query regarding a new point q, we compare q's x-value to the node. If the x-value is greater we search the B subtree and return answer. However, if the point lies in A, we search the left subtree; if it is dominated, we return the dominating point.

If it is not dominated by any point in A, then we must check to see if it is dominated by any point in B. This can be accomplished by storing in each node the maximum y-value of any point in B. This structure can be built in **O(N log N) time** and requires linear space.

Time Complexity

The recurrence relation describing the worst case is:

$$T(N) = T(N/2) + O(1)$$

The worst case for searching is **O(log N)**

k-dimensional all-points maxima

This search structure can be generalized to **k-space**.

A structure representing N points in k-space contains two substructures representing N/2 points in k-space and one substructure representing N/2 points in k-1 space.

To test if a new point is a maximum we first determine if it lies in A or B. If it is in B, then we visit only the right child. If it lies in A, we first see if it is dominated by any point in A ,and if not then we check to see if it is dominated by any point in B (by searching the (k-1)-dimensional structure).

Time Complexity

The recurrences describing the worst-case performance of this structure are

$$P(N, k) = 2P(N/2, k) + P(N, k-1) + O(N),$$

$$S(N, k) = 2S(N/2, k) + S(N/2, k-1) + O(1),$$

$$Q(N, k) = Q(N/2, k) + Q(N/2, k-1) + O(1),$$

which have solutions

$$P(N, k) = O(N \log^{(k-2)} N),$$

$$S(N, k) = O(N \log^{(k-2)} N),$$

$$Q(N, k) = O(\log^{(k-1)} N).$$

Just like the case of the all-points problem, these times are highly pessimistic, and for many point distributions they can be shown to be much less on the average.

Applications of maxima problem

The problem of computing maxima arises in many diverse applications.

Suppose, for example, that we have a set of programs for performing the same task rated on the two dimensions of space efficiency and time efficiency. If we plot these measures as points in the x-y plane, then a point (program) dominates another only if it is more space efficient and more time efficient.

The maximal programs of the set are the only ones we might consider for use, because any other program is dominated by one of the maxima. In general, if we are seeking to maximize some multivariate goodness function (monotone in all variables) over some finite point set, then it suffices to consider only maxima of the set.

This observation can **significantly decrease the cost of optimization** if many optimizations are to be performed. Such computation is common in econometric problems.

1.3) Range Searching

Range Searching as the name suggests is searching for a set of points that are being dominated by two points, let us say U and L, not only are we searching, we also need to answer queries regarding this quickly.

Therefore, we need to build a structure that would facilitate the process. Unlike the previous sections, we do not have a corresponding all-points for this.

This kind of query is usually called an **orthogonal range query** because we are in fact giving for each dimension i a range $R_i = [l_i, u_i]$ and then asking the search to report all points x such that x_i is in range R_i for all i.

One-dimensional range searching

A sorted array can work for this, as the points are in increasing order to answer a query, we have to perform two binary searches on the array to locate the positions of low and high ends of the range.

Once that is done, the points between the range represents the answer.

Time Complexity

The analysis is very similar to our previous analysis

1. **Storage Cost**: linear, O(N)

2. **Query Cost**: binary search, O(log N) + O(F) if a total of F points are found to be in the region

Note that any algorithm for range searching must include a term of O(F) in the analysis of query time.

Two-dimensional range searching

We will be using **range trees** which is an ordered tree data structure to hold a list of points. It allows all the points in each range to be reported efficiently. There are six elements in a range tree's node describing set S. These values are illustrated in the below figure.

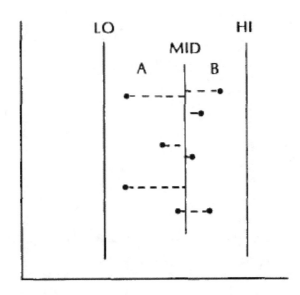

1. The reals LO and HI give the minimum and maximum x-values in the set S (these are accumulated "down" the tree as it is built).

2. The real MID holds the x value defining the line L, which divides S into A and B.

We then store two pointers to range trees representing the sets A and B. The final element stored in the node is a pointer to a sorted array, containing the points of S sorted by y-value.

A range tree can be built recursively in a manner like constructing an ECDF tree. We answer a range query asking for all points with x-value in range X and y-value in range Y by visiting the root of the tree with the following recursive procedure. When visiting node N we compare the range X to the range [LO, HI]. If [LO, HI] is contained in X, then we can do a range search in the sorted array for all points in the range Y (all these points satisfy both the X and Y ranges).

If the X range lies wholly to one side of MID, then we search only the appropriate subtree (recursively); otherwise we search both subtrees.

Time Complexity

The preprocessing costs of this structure and the storage costs are both O(N log N). For the query cost we note that at most two sorted lists are searched at each of the log N levels of the tree, and each of those

---

searches cost at most O(log N), plus the number of points found during that search.

The query cost of this structure is therefore **O(log² N + F)**, where F (as before) is the number of points found in the desired range.

k-dimensional range searching

The range tree structure can be generalized to k-space. Each node in such a range tree contains pointers to two subtrees representing N/2 points in k space and one N point subtree in (k-l)-space.

Time Complexity

Analysis of range trees shows that

```
P(N, k) = O(N log^(k-1) N), S(N, k) = O(N log^(k-1) N)

Q(N, k) = O(log^k N + F)

where F is the number of points found.
```

Applications of Range Searching

A geometric interpretation of the orthogonal range query is that we are asking for all points that lie in each hyper-rectangle.

Such a search might be used in **querying a geographic database to list all cities with latitude between 37 ° and 41° N and longitude between 102 ° and 109 ° W** (this asks for all cities in Colorado). In addition to database problems, range queries are also used in certain statistical applications.

2) Closest-Point Problems

In the previous section we discussed about domination points, here we are going to discuss about closeness. We will be looking into

  1) Fixed-Radius Near Neighbors

  2) Closest Pair

  3) Nearest Neighbors

2.1) Fixed-Radius Near Neighbors

In this section we discuss problems on point sets which deal with absolute closeness of points, that is, pairs of points within some fixed distance d of one another. Just like most of our previous sections we will explore:

1) all-points problem

2) fixed-radius near neighbor searching

2.1.1) All-points problem

We discuss problems on point sets which deal with absolute closeness of points, that is, pairs of points within some fixed distance d of one another.

One-dimensional all-points problem

In this problem we are given N points on a line, constants c and d such that no segment on the line of length 2d contains more than c points, our problem is to list all pairs within d of one another.

We can do this by sorting the points into a list in ascending order and then scanning down that list. When visiting point x during the scan we check backward and forward on the list a distance of d. By the sparsity condition, this involves checking at most c points for "closeness" to x.

Time Complexity

The total cost is O(N log N) which includes O(N log N) for sorting and O(N) for scan.

Note the very important role sparsity plays in analyzing this algorithm: It guarantees that the cost of the scan is linear in N.

Two-dimensional all-points problem

This can be done with the following steps

1. Divide the point set by L into A and B

2. Find all neighbor paths in each recursively. Now we need to find all pairs within d which have one element in A and one in B. Note that the "A point" of such a pair must lie in the slab of A which is within d of L, and likewise for B.

3. Find all pairs with one element in A and the other in B.

The below figure can help you visualize the entire process

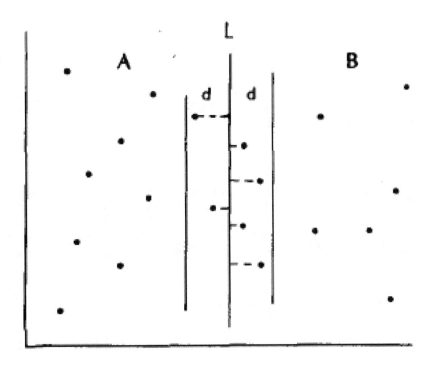

To perform step 3, we need to confine our attention to the slab of width 2d centered about line L. But this can be transformed into a one-dimensional problem by projecting all points in the slab onto L. It is not difficult to show that projection preserves sparsity and it is obvious that projection preserves closeness, for projection only decreases the distance between pairs of points.

Time Complexity

Our reduced problem is therefore just the one-dimensional sparse near neighbor problem (though it requires checking both to ensure pairs have one element from A and one from B and to ensure that the pairs were close before projection). and this can be accomplished in O(N log N) time, or linear time if presorting is used.

The runtime of our algorithm thus obeys the recurrence

$$T(N) = 2T(N/2) + O(N)$$

which has solution T(N) = **O(N log N)**.

Sparsity played two important roles in this algorithm

1) Since the original point set was sparse, we could guarantee that both A and B would be sparse after the division step (which in no way alters A or B).

2) The sparsity condition was also preserved in the projection of the third step, which allowed us to use the one-dimensional algorithm to solve the resulting subproblem.

Three-dimensional all-points problem

The algorithm we just saw can be generalized to three and higher dimensions. In three dimensions we divide the set by a cut plane P into A and B and find all near pairs in those sets recursively.

We now need to find all close pairs with one member in A and the other in B, and to do this we confine our attention to the "slab" of all points within distance d of P.

If we project all those points onto the slab (remembering if each was an A or a B), then we have a planar near neighbor problem of (up to) N points.

Time Complexity

Using our previous planar algorithm gives an algorithm for 3-space with **$O(N \log^2 N)$** running time.

k-dimensional all-points problem

Extending this to k-space gives us an **$O(N \log^{(k-1)} N)$ time algorithm**.

We have seen the above time complexity for many algorithms so far in this book but, do not accept that this is the best time the algorithm can ever accomplish. We can actually do better, and the known lower bound is **$\Omega(N \log N)$**.

First we consider our planar algorithm in its **O(N log² N)** form, temporarily ignoring the speedup available with presorting. The extra logarithmic factor comes from the fact that in the worst case all N points can lie in the slab of width 2d;

This is illustrated in the below figure:

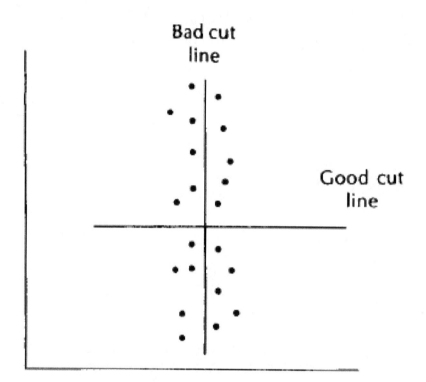

If the points are configured this way, then we should choose as cut line L a horizontal line dividing the set into halves. It turns out not to be hard to generalize this notion to show that in any sparse point set there is a "good" cut line. By "good" we mean that L possesses the following three properties:

1. It is possible to locate L in linear time.

2. The set S is divided approximately in half by L.

3. Only $O(N^{1/2})$ points of S are within d of L.

We can use the existence of such a cut line to create an O(N log N) algorithm.

The first step of our algorithm takes linear time (by property 1 of L), and the second step is altered (by property 2).

The third step is faster because it sorts fewer than N points ,only the $O(N^{1/2})$ points within d of L, by property 3.

Since this can be accomplished in much less than linear time, our algorithm has the recurrence

$$T(N) = 2T(N/2) + O(N)$$

which has solution **O(N log N)**.

The gain in speed was realized here by solving only a very small problem on the fine, so small that it can be solved in much less than linear time. Not unexpectedly, it can be shown that for sparse point sets in k-space there will always exist good cut planes. These planes imply that the (k-1)-dimensional subproblem can be solved in less than linear time, and the full problem thus obeys the recurrence

$$T(N, k) = 2T(N/2, k) + O(N)$$

This establishes that we can solve the general problem in **O(N log N) time**.

2.1.2) Fixed-Radius Near Neighbor Searching

The techniques which we have used for the all-points near neighbors problems can also be applied to the near neighbor searching problem.

In that problem we are given a sparse set of points to preprocess into a data structure such that we can quickly answer queries asking for all points within d of a query point.

If we use the general multidimensional divide-and-conquer strategy, then we achieve a structure very similar to the range tree, with performances

$$P(N) = O(N \log^{(k-1)} N)$$

```
S(N) = O(N log^(k-1) N)

Q(N) = O(log^k N)
```

If we make use of the good cut planes, however, then we can achieve a structure with performance

```
P(N) = O(N log N)

S(N) = O(N)

Q(N) = O(log N)
```

This modified structure follows immediately from the properties of the cut planes we mentioned above; the details are similar to the other multidimensional divide and conquer structures we have seen previously.

To show lower bounds on fixed-radius problems in k-space we can consider the corresponding problems in 1-space.

Studies by Fredman and Weide have shown that the problem of reporting all intersecting pairs among a set of segments on the line requires $\Omega(N \lg N)$ time; by embedding, this immediately gives the same lower bound on the all-points fixed-radius near neighbors problem in k-space.

This shows that our algorithm is **optimal (to within a constant factor)**. Reduction to one-dimensional can also be used to show that the data structure is optimal.

Applications

Fixed-radius problems arise whenever "multidimensional agents" have the capability of affecting all objects within some fixed radius. Such problems arise in:

- air traffic control
- molecular graphics
- pattern recognition
- certain military applications.

2.2) Closest Pair

In this section we examine the closest-pair problem, an all-points problem with no searching analog. We are given N points in k-space and must find the closest pair in the set. Notice that this problem is based on relative, not absolute, distances.

One-dimensional closest pair

First, we need to sort all the points. After performing the sort, we scan through the list, checking the distance between adjacent elements.

Time Complexity

The running time is $O(N \log N)$, which includes $O(N \log N)$ for sorting and $O(N)$ for scanning.

Two-dimensional closest pair

In two dimensions we can use multidimensional divide-and-conquer to solve the problem.

The first step divides S by line L into sets A and B, and the second step finds the closest pairs in A and B, the distances between which we denote by d_a and d_n, respectively. This is illustrated in the below figure.

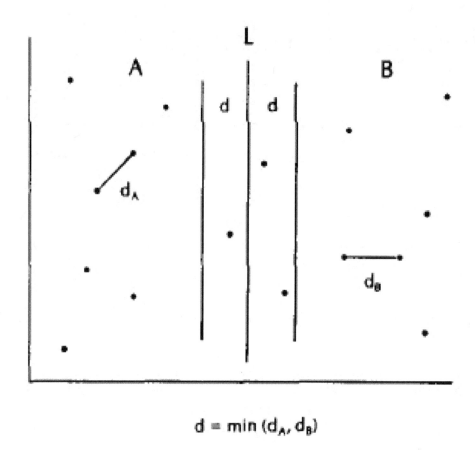

$$d = \min (d_A, d_B)$$

Note that we have now introduced a sparsity condition into both A and B. Because the closest pair in A is d_A apart, no d_A-ball in A can contain more than seven points.

This follows from the fact that at most six-unit circles can be made to touch some fixed unit circle in the plane without overlapping.

Likewise, we can show that B is sparse in the sense that no d_B-ball in B contains more than seven points. If we let d be the minimum of d_A and d_B, notice that the whole space is sparse in the sense that no d-ball contains more than 14 points.

This observation of "induced" sparsity will make the third step of our algorithm much easier, which is to make sure that the closest pair in the space is that corresponding to d_A or to d_B. We could just run a sparse fixed radius near neighbor algorithm at this point to find any pairs within d of one another, but there is a more elegant approach.

Note that any close pair must have one element in A and one element in B, so all we have to do is consider the slab of all points within d of L, and the third step of this algorithm becomes exactly the third step of the near neighbor algorithm.

Time Complexity

The running time without presorting is $O(N \log^2 N)$, if presorting would have been applied the running time is $O(N \log N)$.

Three-dimensional closest pair

We choose a plane P defining A and B and solve the subproblems for those sets. After this we have introduced sparsity into both A and B (relative to d_A and d_B), and we can ensure that our answer is correct by solving a planar fixed radius subproblem.

k-dimensional closest-pair

In k-space we solve two closest-pair problems of N/2 points each in k-space and one fixed-radius problem of (up to) N points in k-1 dimensions.

Time Complexity

If we use the O(N log N) algorithm for near neighbors, then our recurrence is

```
T(N) = 2T(N/2) + O(N log N)
```

which has solution $T(N) = O(N \log^2 N)$. It has been shown that how the good cut planes we saw for the fixed-radius problem can be applied to this problem.

If they are used appropriately, then the running time of the closest-pair algorithm in k-space can be reduced to **O(N log N)**.

2.3) Nearest Neighbors

The final closest-point problem we investigate deals with nearest neighbors. Like most of the previous sections we deal with

1) all-points

2) searching

2.3.1) All-Points Problem

In the all-points form we ask that for each point x the nearest point to x be identified (ties may be broken arbitrarily).

Two-dimensional all-points problem

It is not hard to see how multidimensional divide and conquer can be used to solve the planar problem.

The first step divides S into A and B and the second step finds for each point in A its nearest neighbor in A (and likewise for each point in B).

The third step must "patch up" by finding if any point in A has its true nearest neighbor in B, and similarly for points in B. To aid in this step we observe that we have established a kind of sparsity condition. We define the NNball (for nearest neighbor ball) of point x to be the circle centered at x which has radius equal to the distance from x to x's nearest neighbor.

It can be shown that with this definition no point in the plane is contained in more than seven NN-balls of points in A.

We will now discuss one-half of the third step, namely, the process of ensuring for each point in A that its nearest neighbor in A is actually its nearest neighbor in S.

In this process we need consider only those points in A with NN-balls intersecting the line L (for if their NN-ball did not intersect L, then their nearest neighbor in A is closer than any point in B).

The final step of our algorithm projects all such points of A onto L and then projects every point of B onto L. It is then possible to determine during a linear-time scan of the resulting list if any point x in A has a point in B nearer to x than x's nearest neighbor in A.

Time Complexity

The running time is **O(N log N)** if presorting is used.

k-space all-points problem

The extension of the algorithm to k-space yields $O(N \log^{(k-1)} N)$ performance. It is not clear that there is a search structure corresponding to this algorithm.

Shamos and Lipton and Tarjan have given nearest neighbor search structures for points in the plane that are analogous to this algorithm. Whether there exists a fast k-dimensional nearest neighbor search structure is still an open question.

Applications

The all-points problem has applications in **cluster analysis and multivariate hypothesis testing**; the searching problem arises in **density estimation and classification**.

2.3.2) Searching Problem

In the searching form we give a new point x and ask which of the points in the set is nearest to x. We will not be discussing further into this problem as, mentioned above, it is still an **open question** to find a search structure that would work for the algorithm.

Conclusion

So far, we have discussed many algorithms, starting with describing their problem, building in smaller dimensions, and slowly moving up to obtain a general algorithm. This has been the aim of the paper to build algorithms that general, yet specific to solve a targeted problem.

This book has communicated some of the flavor of the process of algorithm design and analysis, in addition to the nicely packaged results. We hope the reader takes away from this book not only a set of algorithms and data structures, but also a deep understanding of how these objects came into being and the ability to solve a wider range of problems.

iq.opengenus.org

 discuss.opengenus.org

 team@opengenus.org

 amazon.opengenus.org

 linkedIn.opengenus.org

 github.opengenus.org

 twitter.opengenus.org

 facebook.opengenus.org

 instagram.opengenus.org

Feel free to get in touch with us and enjoy learning and solving computational problems.